I0087876

The Knife Collector

Jesse Breite

FUTURECYCLE PRESS

www.futurecycle.org

Published by FutureCycle Press
Hayesville, North Carolina, USA

ISBN 978-1-938853-54-8

For my Sister

"Wherefore by their fruits ye shall know them"
Matthew 7:20, *King James Version*

Contents

Highway 40

An old red truck grumbles over
the dirt road's stiff heat. The trees lob
their branched weight to the West.
An empty beer can glistens sunshine.
A white-tailed hawk perches on a broken fence,
eyeing fat-lettuced fields of mouse and snake.
It's morning in Arkansas. Light spokes
through the plumed clouds. My father's head
rests on a white pillow. He dreams
of the old red truck, the empty beer can.
I watch the land unfold and disappear.
Arkansas is patiently inescapable.
The sharp-eyed king takes to flight—
from its needled claws, illegible shrieking.

Carpenter Ant

He fell off the ceiling, got stuck
marching in the carpet's threaded swamp.
I went for him, but he didn't release
his tonged and chomped jaws.
I gave a quick tug as warning.
On the second, the beaded body
popped free of the ebon head,
and even disembodied, the viced grip
of his chops held fast to the thready bushel.

When members of the family die,
they decide it's going to happen.
My cousin drank holes into
his liver, offering a simple *cheers*
to its failure. His teeth fell out,
one by one. My mom's dad,
who I never knew, smoked sixty
non-filtered cigarettes every day—
his body a furnace of moods.
Grandma said she'd have to
be carried out of the house.
Suddenly, the person disappears.
Only the stubborn jaw echoes after.

Grilling Chicken

In the back, the Weber hisses and pops.
The deck is a heavy-grained brown
beneath our legs. A sweat bee circles
through smoke. Under pine straw,
acidic earth smokelessly chews itself
to woody fingers. Magnolia leaves
grow crisp, breathful, then yellow
to falling. I tong sticky flesh, flip it.
The pulsing grill grits its silver teeth
over the locus of heat. I breathe in
ladled clumps of burnt rosemary. I hear
roots crackling through ground.

Driving Mississippi

into Arkansas. Water in the bean fields
glints symmetrical and gold,
row-by-row. The Delta-folk leave
yards littered with rusted car parts,
stained mattresses, boatless boat hitches.

An old man sits out back on a cold,
hard-worn surface
and hums out assumptions. I hear him
through counties. I see him in the water.

My foot tingles to an ache.
My arm holds the wheel's steady slip.
And I recognize it: this dither in the nerves,
the weight of thinking, or not.

An oak tree silhouettes in fields.
It creeps toward the highway,
branching through air,
to claim something, someone.

The Knife Collector

Monday night, I sprain my ankle
playing ball. And I keep playing.
At my place, my foot swells brown
around the heel, black in the toes.

Mom calls. Her voice is afraid.
It's Jane, again. She hasn't come home
in days. Last time, they found her
emptied car before picking her up.

At three a.m., I wake up, take a piss,
feel blood stutter down my leg,
through the lumped bruises. Back in bed,
my foot throbs like a dying fish.

The log of my body writhes over
a dull fire spreading nervously.
I curse until it eases, enough
to sleep.
            I dream of my father
and his knife collection. Each one
with a smooth handle—whale bone
or steel, bearing alien monograms.
He sits on a squeaky wooden chair,
chews Red Man, hones a warm blade.
He spits and says, *Keep this here fine,*
and you won't even feel it go through.

Soft Trains

The trains riddle through, just
around midnight. You can hear
them through the walls.
They rumble like steel hounds
on a crimson scent.
In bed, I hear the air mostly,
birds lost in Atlanta, sometimes
the neighbors having sex.
I spend hours listening.
Emily breathes, her body
rises, falls. Again, a train
blows up the spinal column.
And I think of how soft it can be,
feeling a train—not like
Blanche Dubois turning head-on
into her past—just clunky, tooled
blood rushing through the body.

Make Good of the Dead

No one wants to say things about the boy
or the girl or the man because
the molded face in the open casket
is dead and looks dead.

We wander around the empty room
searching for old conversations we had
with the deceased, but it could be years
if we decide to dig up that grave.

Fir trees know how to make good of the dead
by fingering through softened, fibrous skin
(as if grasping for the heart)
and unabashedly growing up out of a corpse.

And who knows better than the moss,
that bejeweled, pubic robe crawling over
the naked trunk, crotch and limbs of the dead?
Moss, you second skin, spell the bronze

stones of the earth into the fecund howl,
cracking forth, beaming—light (O God) into light.

Animal

In the sudden light on the back porch,
I follow a magnified shadow crawling
over the wall. A matted tail waddles darkly.
Moving to the window, I see a raccoon
wearing stale fur like an unwashed dress.
He turns to me—his black eyes cut
from obsidian glowering to hold
my windowed silhouette. How easy
he is with his wild grit, his feral nonchalance,
as he turns again to slide his fluid body
through a notched opening beneath
the porch. Back in the bedroom,
Emily pulls and drops her bright clothes.
Shadows exaggerate glowing skin.
Her touch is brief, furry. Strange light
sprinkles into the river where we drink.

Easter Morning

Running along the road in Northwest Atlanta,
I observe a mother possum and her babes
strung across the curb as the high-velocity dead.

Red blood, even from the babes, is the tell that
they don't play. I turn away, but there is justice
in the kill—a clean massacre. No child left

to clean it up; no father to give the obligation of
meaning, or take-away. And though
confused by the cruelties of death, I understand

something tender in the steel relieving
this furried eagerness and her baby urgencies
of rodent work. I slow to a walk, recall

the body, and hear a voiceless stirring
in a wood beside the road.

Calumet Ritual, Little Rock 1997

All you could see from the big rock deep
in Meriwether Park—a cherry of fire
going up, down, across the horizon of us.

Smoky calligraphy hoisted into the sky
as we spoke by bloodshot surfaces,
muddled body and motion. Common spirit

spidered down through instinct,
rooting us: skin callous to stone, dirt,
to the strange lines of counties.

On the river, La Harpe must've felt that
this place—where the Delta births foothills—
might be where men too could change landscape:

that creatures, ceremonial in the waiting dark,
could displace, ripple forth, alter-bloom.

Firefly

Jane slow-steps around the driveway
inhaling the glow of a smoke. She dances
like she did when we were young
at her seven three-hour dance recitals
Mom made me attend in slacks.
She twirls around the smoked butts,
dead as bullet shells on stone.
It's one hundred and six degrees
in Little Rock. I sit on the stone porch
watching. I shout, but Jane smolders
deaf. The sun plunges through pine.
Darkness surrounds her lightning bob.
She imagines her burn as that of the sky.
Exhaling, her ruddy face glows bright,
only for this brief, wandering night.

Outside the Garden

I hear her little sentence on the phone, distant.
A male voice lashes, buckles underneath hers.
She whispers out secrets: her divorce is final.
This is her job: dirty laundry, another bed, cash
that was and is still under the table—nothing
she can explain. In the picture that's sent to
my phone, she weighs thirty pounds less than
three months ago. I wonder how she understands
this reshaping of her clay. She's her own child,
her own mother, tilling her fields after a dead season,
letting her legs tilt and shiver in the wind.
On her bright red skin, quaking buds set and shake.
A marvelous eye ignites her soft, buoyant petals.
I'm a breath short of knowing, pitifully unatoned.

Contrition

My father doesn't understand—
why my sister puts a needle into
her bloodstream to feel feelings.

He is of old St. Louis, its slow alleys,
its crawling river. Pistols, he gets,
and Budweisers, what burns under

the hood of a Ford, but not this fine
specimen of hypermagical continuous.
Dad sees things plain and stubborn,

not with my distant, simple eyes,
not with Mom's potent shame.
I want to write the story easier

than silence, in the soft language
of greeting or fridge magnets, so even
grandparents and cousins can get it.

I see students every day. I wonder
where their simple, logical choices
will lead them. I drive the roads

to work in Atlanta. They're beaten
shit-brown and hard black. They're ready,
I think. I hear the hurt in Mom's voice.

Dad says, *Please, I don't often talk about it.*
And Jane, she is the poorest of spirit.
This, I tell him, *is what it means to be blessed.*

Oxycontin

March '94, Swiss vets first tested OC
on living things before it pilled the market
in '96. Purdue Pharma took millions
binding opioid receptors to euphoria
in the continuous relief of feelings.
July '01, *The New York Times* dubbed it
hillbilly heroin. A regional problem,
they called it. Then Limbaugh headlined.
Now my sister, sobered from a jail cell,
withdraws at home. Her body quakes as she lies.
24 hours away, Mom cries
into my aloof ear from a Nokia cell.
Lock her up is what I decide to say.
Lock her up or she will run away.

The Cardinal

Back home, a single male cardinal
hurls its feathered body
against the living room's plated glass
again.

First, I thought he wanted cool shelter,
or perhaps he misunderstood air.
But Mom says he sees his reflection
and thinks it's an intruder.
He is his one fear, his only enemy.
Dad calls him *the dipshit bird.*
Mom says *He's at it again.*

When Jane loses a job, she doesn't call back.
Mom says she hasn't seen her in a week.
Dad says he knows she's trying.

The three of us sit in the living room.
We see her fret through scraps to recraft her soul.
Then, the heavy thud.
Mom moves to get up, but Dad stops her.

The Diamond State

Used to sit out in Newp Park,
smoking after class.
Bobby'd roll down the street,
bring back 40s. Nothing moved
but when we taught it to.

Jane took the same route to Newp,
but a man put a gun to her head,
took her keys, blew up her car,
left it by the river.

I've wondered what it was like
to have a revolver to the head—
how it would feel to stomach
illogical hatred, necessary pills.

Dad thought she believed
she deserved what happened.
Though she offered *Okay* and *Fine,*
she didn't say *Leave me be.*

I should've talked more, told her
I know I'm not who she is,
but panning through Arkansas dirt,
you're bound to find
hard guilt, rare wisdom—uncut.

Even if I couldn't put it into words,
I should've said it anyway.

Being My Age

I've made decisions that I'll never tell my father.
I wonder what would change if he was my age?
What would his jaw never give? Sex impulse,
alcoholic demand, fears stitched to breathing.
Would he be the one I'd take a black eye from?

Keith called me once from jail, wanted to be
picked up. I knew. No words. I wasn't father.
I drove over, signed the paper, walked back
to the truck first, let him open his own door,
listened to the air whisper over the windows
on the drive back, told him that I'd see him later
without thinking, its torrent of luxuries.

Hell's Half Acre—

what grayshirts called Little Rock
during the war. Off the river, downtown,

a soldier could find a good whore
who never ran out of tart

and a drink that burnt real cool.
Keith, Bobby and I blaze over

the riverfront under the same heavenly stones
and find a similar menu.

Hours later, Bobby spits out a tooth.
Keith drops an iron heel on Cantrell Road.

Behind, night shimmers blue and white.
I greet a new lady at a stoplight:

Well hello there pretty, what's your name?

Locusts and Honey

The doctor says my sister tears her skin
because she sees bugs. Her nails shovel
through her body until it spurts blossoms.
Along the gutter's underbelly, I spot
the transparent loaf of a shell split open.
I climb a ladder, pluck its molt off the house.
Somewhere this released spirit crows
mysteries—sacred through its cedar throat.
I marvel at glimmering thorax, its distant voice.
She sits in a cold room, prying herself open.
In the kitchen, I turn off the light, burn candles,
anoint with honey and tongue the heavy gem.

The Land of Opportunity

Pity them all:
the trailer-burbs of tooth-rot
and beer-rust;
the nostalgic dreamers of lake-fish,
river-blood,
of bodies ripe, floating with feeling;
the tattooed—pale-skinned,
clock-headed;
all those exiting the century—they
were in love
with their own shocking selves,
their impossible language
from Bentonville to Magnolia to West Memphis.

And pardon the thousand sons of Fayetteville
buying up exams,
failing their way into seven-digit money.
The pills they've bartered.
They never bothered
to read their histories, never back-paddled
through apocryphal counties.
And once they lived long enough,
proved they could
stubborn the dirt, we let them settle,
tied our parts together
with their parts—we became opportune.

And spare the money, the diamonds, the business
of Walmart, Tyson, JB Hunt,
the old sagging country-club bodies roosting

in Hot Springs—
what they've taken and what they allow.
The hands that pan out
an existence.
The sellers of fridge magnets, wolf art.
The buyers,
the quarter-gamblers in truck stops,
the sweaty hot dog feeders.
The columns steeped in secrecies,
the gilded door frames, the claret-gold mailbox flags,
the young presidents.
The smoothly spoken, how they—how we
have said it aloud
and believed it and made others believe
despite untruths.

And forgive the abuse, the inheritance
of abusers, of molesters,
of sons, daughters
alone in the houses of naked men,
the impulse to consume one's self with deservings,
beaten down, passed around—
re-directed blame.
Forgive the apathetic rubber of dolls and cribs.
The smoking mothers on the porch.
The recognition
is long, hard, cracked concrete. You feel every slab
of the highway—you
spine-guilty Arkansawyer.

And mercy for testimony, the witness that says
it is or it isn't so:
what always comes back to infected visions,
the haunting—which we will
be unable to remember as action or inaction
but always

eternal, ubiquitous truth, like blood
and the horse within
from which we derive our teeth, our teething,
our whetting.

And mercy for the stones, the trees, the tar creeks
that cannot move,
that must bear the weight of Quapaw territory,
calumet ritual,
the cottonmouths that wrap our bones,
the pig-nosed
turtles chewing our tender, spare flesh.
Mercy for everything
with or without language. Let us revive
obscurity—
and the gentle, righteous choices made.

Pity the captain sailing down the river,
the one who saw
and summoned it into being: *Le Petit Rocher.*
The fetus buried in the soil,
its industrial roots.
When, oh wind, will you carry off
this terrible fruit
from the dirt, fraught with stone?
The alligator eye
squints into being. All this was just to ask
you, old visitor,
where it is you think you'd like to rest?

Fishing in the Dark

Language is a fickle thing. It'd be easier
if crafted with an alphabet of disappointments.
Imagine that—not this
horsefly's drama of settling onto the surface,
being so sure of what is or isn't under the water.

Dad took me fishing in the dark
on the banks of Lake Dardanelle many times
in Arkansas. We caught sunfish like liquid prisms—
golden mirrors—in our palms
and threw them back to the lake's glass mouth.

I can still feel crickets crawling over
my little hands, deep in the cricket-cage,
and the gristle of worms my father tore
and fleshed apart on dirty metal.

We drove Highway 7 in the black Nissan truck.
Dad handled the stick, shifting it firmly
into the engine's argument. The spin of the passing
woods unveiled landscapes. The water settled
into gravity, and it rippled, licking at the wind.

Inference can be so nightmarish, sinister
as lightning forked into the nerves.
You have to enlist the harder parts, suggest
the silence and let it be silence, learn to slide
a wriggling thing onto the sun-full, jag-lipped silver.

Even then, what's strung snags on
what's available—logs floating through water—
and only the surrounding feelings change
what's double-fisted above your lungs.

The Most Beautiful Wolf

runs over spinal ridges. She's been spotted
in Gentry, Rodgers, Bella Vista.

Tracks measured at five by four, her coming
and going is nakedly undetectable.

Overhead, a red-tailed hawk flies
as satellite to the most beautiful wolf.

Between is corn-dust, fiber-needle
mapping the air spiritual.

Gray blur gnawing into blue sky,
she moves liquid as dolphin-shadow.

Her hair grows of the old man's nose;
her eyes gleam sun, puddle on a Magnolia leaf.

Her teeth strike, the flash of knives turning
into flesh: skin-lacera and blood-swamp.

At her tooth-end, your spirit will rise.

Two Rivers

By the willow, I used to take bamboo
and line to hook mudcats at the confluence.

Jane made wildflower wreaths.
Dad watched small boats beat the water.
The barges slugged by, burnished
by the sun. Tall grass arched swan-like

into pitiful bowing. Now, I dream of
children pouring bottles into gardens,
urgent light in the heavily breathed dark,
a marble sky mirrored in the river.

The tumescent river folds together.
A captain rows in the driftwood boat.
Joe and Luke swim naked in the water;
their shapes are fleshy and mechanic.

Behind, two fetal heaps limb out—
one red, the other grasps at his heel.
The captain picks up spent coils
floating, tosses them back.

Years after, Dad's gone blind.
Mom bakes up his chosen dish.
Jane serves him the plate of meat.
He blesses her with the smell of fields,

with the glistening dew. I come back
to Little Rock, and I bow down
at her feet. I pluck the blood orange
from my chest, shuffle off its peel.

I offer it by a sapient palm.

70 East, Monroe County

The highway crests out of low land,
crowned on either side by naked trees.
They spike and lumber, wretched
as the Memphis blues.
The earth wets with risen water.
Hieroglyphic terrains submerge.
Light pours through cirrus haze.
Snowmelt trickles into breath-blood.
I think of the year as prismatic,
fat light blunting colors to brevity.
Emily says she waited for me.
Histories churn in atmospheric sciences,
dirty puddles, leaf-meal, weed-root.
The land gallops through my chest—
its hills and grasses. I absorb
kinetic chronicles. The textures
of generations thicken into my skin.
I feel the urgencies of old men, women,
crooked mountains, road grit, empty cans.
Suddenly, as if retrograde, out of me:
a speeding pickup truck heaves past.
It's a black-silver planet of gravities.
I wonder how one escapes the past
and its animals, outruns inevitable stops?
Rainwater flares up angelic behind
the wheels, enveloping its muscle.
Into the road's horizon, it squints out,
while the Arkansas earth eats what it can.

The Centurion

On a dark New Year's, I raised a sparkler
in the Peabody down on West Markham,
kissing every girl I could reach out and grab,
kissing the end of each champagne bottle,
kissing the end of the century one last time
before leaving the only century I will have left.
I woke up yesterday with the hangover.

Every day I wake up with a headache—
rod-like, lividly whitish, crucifix-faced.
I'm tired of being a creature of repetition:
the grunted waking, scream of the news,
class-whirl, bone-work, brain-spin.
Retrospection settles into a skin-full dust.

The expert on Shakespeare says I should
teach the experience.
I begin again reclaiming syllables.

He says to start with bit of a garden,
put up gates—don't let anyone in or out.
Anoint the body, spinning forward
and back. Stomp the moistened ground;

let it come back, sprouting through
the heel, vining up, leafing off veins,
blowing through the spinal trunk,
bursting the skull's fault lines.

Then, he says, walk around
the furious planet as if it were a peach.

Acknowledgments

These journals first published a version of the following poems:

The Nashville Review: "The Knife Collector," "Locusts and Honey"
Prairie Schooner: "Contrition"
Southern Poetry Anthology, Volume V: Georgia: "Highway 40"
The Natural Tale: "Hell's Half-Acre"
Town Creek Poetry: "Carpenter Ant," "Make Good of the Dead,"
     "Outside the Garden," "Being My Age," "The Land of Opportunity,"
     "The Most Beautiful Wolf," "70 East, Monroe County"

*Cover photo by Jesse Breite; author photo by Emily Breite; cover
and interior book design by Diane Kistner (dkistner@futurecycle.org);
DejaVu Sans Condensed text with Agency FB titling*

About FutureCycle Press

FutureCycle Press is dedicated to publishing lasting English-language poetry and flash fiction books, chapbooks, and anthologies in both print-on-demand and ebook formats. Founded in 2007 by long-time independent editor/publishers and partners Diane Kistner and Robert S. King, the press incorporated as a nonprofit in 2012. A number of our editors are distinguished poets and writers in their own right, and we have been actively involved in the small press movement going back to the early seventies.

The FutureCycle Poetry Book Prize and honorarium is awarded annually for the best full-length volume of poetry we publish in a calendar year. Introduced in 2013, our Good Works projects are devoted to issues of universal significance, with all proceeds donated to a related worthy cause. Our Selected Poems series highlights contemporary poets with a substantial body of work to their credit. Our flash fiction line presents quick reads that can be serious or light-hearted, irreverent or quirky, fantastic or futuristic, or just plain fun.

We are dedicated to giving all of the authors we publish the care their work deserves, making our catalog of titles the most diverse and distinguished it can be, and paying forward any earnings to fund more great books. We've learned a few things about independent publishing over the years. We've also evolved a unique, resilient publishing model that allows us to focus mainly on vetting and preserving for posterity the most books of exceptional quality without becoming overwhelmed with bookkeeping and mailing, fundraising activities, or taxing editorial and production "bubbles." To find out more, come see us at www.futurecycle.org.